HOW TO GROW CARE MANAGE AND USE RADICCHIO FOR PROFIT

Once Touch Guide To Profitable
Radicchio Farming For Sustainable
Small Business Growth And
Entrepreneurial Success In Agriculture

LARRY NANCY

CHAPTER ONE   7

INTRODUCTION TO RADICCHIO   7
Definition And Origins Of Radicchio   7
Varieties Of Radicchio   8
Historical Significance: 8

CHAPTER TWO   10

UNDERSTANDING THE MARKET   10
Market Trends And Demand For Radicchio   10
Identifying Target Customers   11

CHAPTER THREE   13

PLANNING YOUR RADICHIO FARM   13
Climate Considerations: 13
Budget And Financial Planning   14
Growing And Managing Radicchio   15
Seed Selection And Propagation   15
Crop Rotation With Companion Planting   16
Control Of Insects And Diseases   16
Harvesting And Handling After Harvest   17
Optimal Harvest Timing: 18
Post-Harvest Handling And Storage   18
Market Access And Distribution Channels   18

CHAPTER FOUR   20

RADICCHIO CULTIVATION TECHNIQUES   20

CHAPTER FIVE   24

PEST AND DISEASE MANAGEMENT   24
Disease Prevention And Control Measures   25
Solutions For Organic Pest Management   26

CHAPTER SIX   28

CROP MAINTENANCE AND CARE   28
Pruning And Thinning   28
Weed Control Methods   29
Monitor Plant Health   29
Seasonal Care Guidelines   30

CHAPTER SEVEN   31

HARVESTING RADICCHIO FOR OPTIMAL QUALITY   31
Determining The Right Harvest Time   31
Harvesting Techniques   32
Post-Harvest Handling And Storage   32
.   32

CHAPTER EIGHT   35

ADDING VALUE TO YOUR RADICCHIO   35
Creating Unique Radicchio Products   35
Marketing Strategies For Value-Added Radicchio.   36
Organic Radicchio Farming   36
Water Conservation In Radicchio Crops   37

CHAPTER NINE   39

FINANCIAL MANAGEMENT AND RECORD-KEEPING   39
Expense And Budget Monitoring   39
Revenue Recording   40

CHAPTER TEN   43

RECIPES AND CULINARY USES FOR RADICCHIO   43

CONCLUSION   44

"How to Grow, Care, Manage, and Use Radicchio for Profit" is a comprehensive guide that delves into the multifaceted world of cultivating and profiting from Radicchio, a unique and versatile crop. The book begins with an insightful introduction to radicchio, giving readers a foundational understanding of the plant and its potential.

Understanding the market is a critical aspect of any successful venture, and this book devotes an entire chapter to equipping readers with the knowledge needed to navigate the market dynamics surrounding Radicchio. Planning your radicchio farm is a strategic process, and the book provides valuable insights into effective planning techniques that maximize yield and profit.

The book's chapters on radicchio cultivation techniques, pest and disease management, crop maintenance, and care serve as a practical manual for both new and experienced farmers, providing actionable advice to ensure a healthy and thriving radicchio crop.

Radicchio harvesting is a critical step in the process, and the book provides detailed guidance on when and how to harvest for the best results.

It also goes beyond cultivation by exploring ways to add value to your radicchio, allowing farmers to maximize their profits through innovative approaches.

Financial management and record-keeping are critical components of any successful agricultural venture, and this guide addresses these issues in a separate chapter, providing practical advice for ensuring the financial viability and sustainability of radicchio farming enterprises.

Finally, a chapter on recipes and culinary uses of radicchio broadens the book's appeal beyond farmers to chefs, food enthusiasts, and consumers interested in incorporating this unique ingredient into their culinary repertoire.

Overall, "How to Grow, Care, Manage, and Use Radicchio for Profit" is an indispensable resource that not only empowers farmers with the knowledge needed for successful radicchio cultivation but also opens up new avenues for culinary

CHAPTER ONE
INTRODUCTION TO RADICCHIO

Radicchio, scientifically known as Cichorium intybus, is a leafy vegetable belonging to the chicory genus. Originally cultivated in Italy, radicchio has gained popularity worldwide for its culinary versatility and potential for profitable cultivation. This vegetable is a member of the Asteraceae family, and its cultivation and utilization have evolved significantly over the years.

Definition And Origins Of Radicchio

Radicchio, derived from the Italian "radicchio" meaning chicory, is a type of leaf chicory that undergoes a unique growth process, resulting in tight, compact heads of colorful leaves. The origins of radicchio can be traced back to ancient times, with evidence suggesting its cultivation by the ancient Egyptians and Greeks. However, it wasn't until the Renaissance in Italy that radicchio gained prominence, particularly in the Veneto region.

Varieties Of Radicchio

Radicchio comes in many different varieties, each with its distinct color, size, and flavor. The most well-known are Chioggia, Treviso, and Castelfranco. Chioggia radicchio has a deep red color and a compact head, with a bold, bitter flavor. Treviso radicchio, on the other hand, has elongated, wineglass-shaped heads and a milder taste than Chioggia radicchio. Castelfranco radicchio

Historical Significance:

Radicchio's historical significance is deeply rooted in its cultivation and consumption patterns, particularly in Italy. The vegetable's journey from being a regional specialty to a global culinary sensation reflects changes in agricultural practices, culinary preferences, and international trade. In the Veneto region, where radicchio cultivation thrived, the vegetable became a symbol of local identity and a source of economic prosperity. Radicchio transcended over time

Radicchio, with its origins deeply intertwined with Mediterranean history, has evolved into a versatile and sought-after vegetable that caters to varying culinary preferences, offering opportunities for strategic cultivation and market positioning.

CHAPTER TWO
UNDERSTANDING THE MARKET

Radicchio, a leafy vegetable with a distinctive bitter taste, has seen a surge in popularity in recent years, particularly in gourmet and health-conscious markets. An analysis of market trends reveals a growing demand for unique and flavorful produce, positioning radicchio as an appealing option for both consumers and chefs. To embark on a successful journey in radicchio cultivation for profit, a thorough understanding of the market is paramount.

Market Trends And Demand For Radicchio

Radicchio's unique bitter flavor profile, coupled with a rich burgundy color, makes it stand out in the culinary landscape. As the awareness of the

Potential Profitability of Radicchio Cultivation:

Radicchio cultivation has a high market value due to its scarcity compared to other vegetables, making it an appealing option for farmers looking for niche markets. If approached strategically and informedly, radicchio cultivation can be profitable.

Identifying Target Customers

To successfully cultivate and profit from radicchio, a clear identification of target customers is required. These customers include both end consumers and intermediate buyers such as restaurants, grocery stores, and specialty markets. Understanding the preferences and purchasing behavior of these diverse customer segments is pivotal. High-end restaurants, for example, may seek top-quality, aesthetically pleasing radicchio to enhance the visual appeal of their dishes, w

In conclusion, farmers can position themselves for success in the competitive and lucrative world of radicchio production by aligning cultivation practices with market preferences, identifying target customers, and staying attuned to changing trends. This requires a multifaceted understanding of the market, which includes current trends, demand dynamics, and potential profitability.

CHAPTER THREE
PLANNING YOUR RADICHIO FARM

A successful radicchio farm requires careful consideration of a variety of criteria to ensure maximum growth and profitability, including site selection and soil preparation, climate concerns, budgeting, and financial planning.

Site Selection and Soil Preparation:

Radicchio thrives in well-drained, fertile soils with a pH range of 6.0 to 7.5, and prefers slightly acidic to neutral soils with a pH range of 6.0 to 7.5. Radicchio requires ample sunlight for proper growth and development, so choose a site with good sunlight exposure. Proper soil preparation is also important.

Climate Considerations:

Radicchio is a cool-season crop that thrives in temperatures ranging from 50°F to 70°F (10°C to

21°C), so choose a region with a climate that aligns with these temperature requirements.

Radicchio's characteristic red color and flavor are enhanced by adequate sunlight and cool temperatures. Keep in mind that potential frost dates, such as late spring or e

Budget And Financial Planning

To ensure the long-term viability and profitability of your radicchio farm, create a comprehensive budget and financial plan. Begin by estimating the costs associated with land acquisition or lease, soil preparation, seeds or seedlings, irrigation systems, and any necessary infrastructure.

Consider ongoing expenses such as fertilizers, pest control measures, and labor, as well as overhead costs like equipment maintenance, utilities, and marketing. Accurate

Growing And Managing Radicchio

Seed selection and propagation, crop rotation and companion planting, pest and disease management.

To maintain a healthy and robust crop, successful radicchio production requires careful seed selection and propagation, as well as appropriate crop rotation and companion planting strategies, and pest and disease management.

Seed Selection And Propagation

Choosing the right radicchio variety is a critical decision that can significantly impact the success of your farm. When selecting radicchio seeds, consider factors such as climate suitability, disease resistance, and market demand. Opt for reputable seed suppliers to ensure high-quality, viable seeds. Proper propagation methods, whether through direct seeding or transplanting, play a vital role in the early stages of radicchio growth.

Crop Rotation With Companion Planting

To prevent soil-borne diseases and maintain soil fertility, it is critical to implement a sound crop rotation plan.

To minimize the risk of diseases that may affect radicchio, avoid planting it in the same location consecutively. Rotate radicchio with other crops that have different nutrient requirements to balance soil health. Companion planting entails strategically placing plants that mutually benefit each other.

Control Of Insects And Diseases

Integrated pest management (IPM) strategies, which combine cultural, biological, and chemical control methods, are essential for successful radicchio cultivation. Regular monitoring of the crop for signs of pests and diseases is essential for early intervention.

Encourage natural predators that prey on common radicchio pests, such as aphids or caterpillars.

Use organic pesticides when necessary to minimize environmental impact.

Harvesting And Handling After Harvest

Optimal harvesting timing, post-harvest handling and storage, market access, and distribution channels.

Efficient harvesting and post-harvest handling practices are critical for preserving the quality of radicchio, extending its shelf life, and ensuring successful market access. Paying attention to optimal harvesting timing, post-harvest handling, and selecting appropriate distribution channels are key considerations in this stage of radicchio farming.

Optimal Harvest Timing:

To avoid rot and disease, harvest radicchio heads when they are firm and compact, with vibrant coloration, and before they become overly mature and bitter. The best time to harvest radicchio depends on the variety of radicchio that is being grown.

Post-Harvest Handling And Storage

To keep radicchio fresh and marketable, post-harvest handling is crucial. After harvesting, remove any damaged or undesirable leaves and trim the root ends. Wash the heads carefully to remove soil and debris and allow them to dry thoroughly before packaging. Proper packaging is crucial for protecting radicchio during transportation and storage. Consider using breathable packaging materials to prevent condensation and reduce

Market Access And Distribution Channels

A successful radicchio farming operation depends on establishing effective market access and selecting appropriate distribution channels. Identify potential buyers, such as local grocery stores, farmers' markets, restaurants, or distributors, and establish relationships to secure reliable market outlets. Consider diversifying your distribution channels to reach a broader consumer base. Direct-to-consumer sales via farmers' markets or community support

Growing, caring for, managing, and utilizing radicchio for profit requires a holistic and strategic approach. From the initial planning stages, including site selection and soil preparation, climate considerations, and budgeting, to the cultivation and management phases, which include seed selection, crop rotation, pest and disease management, and finally, harvesting, post-harvest handling, and market access—each aspect plays a crucial role in the overall

CHAPTER FOUR
RADICCHIO CULTIVATION TECHNIQUES

Seed Selection and Propagation: The success of a radicchio cultivation venture begins with the careful selection of high-quality seeds. Seed quality directly impacts the germination rate, plant vigor, and overall crop yield. For optimal results, it is advisable to choose seeds from reputable suppliers with a proven track record in providing genetically pure and disease-free radicchio seeds. Before sowing, growers should consider factors such as seed viability, purity, an

When radicchio seedlings reach an appropriate size, usually four to six weeks after germination, they are ready to be transplanted to the field.

The spacing between radicchio plants should be carefully considered to optimize resource utilization and prevent competition for nutrients and sunlight.

Irrigation and Water Management: Because radicchio prefers well-drained, moist soil conditions, effective irrigation and water management play a pivotal role in ensuring optimal growth and preventing stress-induced issues. Drip irrigation systems are frequently favored for radicchio cultivation because they provide controlled and consistent moisture levels, minimizing the risk of water-related diseases and optimizing water use efficiency. It is essential to monitor

Radicchio has specific nutrient requirements, particularly in terms of nitrogen, phosphorus, and potassium, so developing an effective fertilization strategy is critical for maximizing yield and quality. Soil testing is an essential first step in determining nutrient deficiencies and guiding fertilizer application decisions. Organic amendments, such as compost and well-rotted manure, can enhance soil structure and nutrient content.

Harvesting and Post-Harvest Management: Radicchio's flavor, texture, and market value are significantly influenced by the timing of its harvest. Harvesting is typically done when the heads reach full maturity, which is characterized by well-formed, compact hearts and vibrant coloration. Care should be taken to avoid damaging the outer leaves during harvest, as this can impact the marketability of the produce. Efficient post-harvest handling involves immediate cooling to preserve the product.

Radicchio cultivation is susceptible to various pests and diseases that can compromise crop health and yield. Integrated pest management (IPM) practices are essential for sustainable pest control, emphasizing biological, cultural, and chemical control measures. Regular monitoring of the field for signs of pests or diseases allows early intervention, reducing the need for extensive chemical treatments. Companion planting with beneficial plants

Market Strategies and Profitability: To maximize profitability in radicchio cultivation, a well-thought-out market strategy is imperative. Understanding market demand, identifying target consumers, and establishing effective distribution channels are key components. Direct marketing avenues, such as farmers' markets and community-supported agriculture (CSA) programs, can create a direct connection with consumers and enhance product visibility. Collaborating with local grocery stores, restaurants, and specialty markets provides additional avenues for market penetration. Emphasizing the unique qualities of radicchio, such as its distinct bitter flavor and nutritional benefits, can be a compelling selling point. Implementing sustainable and organic cultivation practices aligns with consumer preferences, contributing to a positive brand image and potentially commanding premium prices in the market. Continuous market research and adaptation to consumer trends are essential for long-term success in the radicchio cultivation business.

CHAPTER FIVE
PEST AND DISEASE MANAGEMENT

Radicchio cultivation for profit necessitates a thorough grasp of pest and disease management to assure optimal yields and quality. Common pests that affect radicchio constitute a substantial danger to the crop, and effective control strategies are critical for successful cultivation.

Common pests affecting radicchio:

In radicchio cultivation, dealing with common pests that can inflict damage on the crop is one of the primary challenges. Aphids, for example, are a prevalent threat, feeding on the plant's sap and transmitting viral diseases. Their rapid reproduction and ability to colonize plants make them a formidable adversary for radicchio growers. Additionally, flea beetles can cause extensive damage by chewing small holes in leaves, compromising the overall health of the planet.

Crop rotation to disrupt pest life cycles, the introduction of natural predators like ladybugs, and the use of insecticidal soaps are all part of a comprehensive approach to pest control in radicchio cultivation. Integrated pest management (IPM) strategies, which combine cultural, biological, and chemical control methods, are essential for mitigating the impact of these pests.

Disease Prevention And Control Measures

Fungal diseases like powdery mildew and downy mildew, which thrive in humid conditions, pose a significant threat to radicchio crops, affecting both yield and quality. To reduce the risk of disease outbreaks, good agricultural practices, such as proper sanitation and hygiene, must be followed.

In addition to cultural practices, the use of disease-resistant radicchio varieties can be an effective strategy. Selecting varieties with inherent resistance to common diseases reduces the reliance on chemical interventions. When fungicides and bactericides are deemed necessary, they should be applied judiciously and under recommended guidelines to prevent the development of resistance and minimize environmental impact.

Solutions For Organic Pest Management

Many radicchio growers are adopting organic pest management methods, which emphasize sustainability and environmental stewardship while maintaining the crop's economic viability. Biological control agents, such as predatory insects and parasitoids, help regulate pest populations without the use of synthetic chemicals.

Neem oil, derived from the neem tree, is a popular organic pesticide that can effectively control a variety of pests without leaving harmful residues. Another key principle in organic farming is crop diversity, which can be used to disrupt pest cycles and create a more balanced ecosystem. Planting companion species that repel pests or attract beneficial insects contributes to a healthier radicchio crop.

In conclusion, successful radicchio cultivation for profit hinges on adept pest and disease management. By understanding the common pests affecting radicchio, implementing disease prevention measures, and adopting organic pest management solutions, growers can safeguard their crops and optimize yields in an environmentally sustainable manner.

CHAPTER SIX
CROP MAINTENANCE AND CARE

Radicchio, a popular green vegetable, necessitates precise crop maintenance and care for optimal development and profitability. When it comes to crop management, several fundamental themes emerge as critical success factors.

Pruning And Thinning

Pruning and thinning are essential practices in radicchio cultivation, affecting both plant health and overall yield. Pruning involves removing unwanted or damaged foliage, which promotes air circulation and reduces the risk of disease. Thinning, on the other hand, focuses on spacing plants appropriately, ensuring ample room for growth and efficient resource utilization. Pruning and thinning should be executed judiciously, considering the specific rad.

Weed Control Methods

Weed control is critical in radicchio cultivation because unchecked weed growth can compete for nutrients, water, and sunlight, ultimately compromising yield and quality.

It is recommended to use a combination of cultural, mechanical, and chemical weed control methods. Culturally, mulching and cover cropping can suppress weed growth. Mechanically, regular cultivation and hand weeding are essential for removing weeds without damaging the radicchio root.

Monitor Plant Health

Early detection of pest infestations, disease symptoms, and nutrient deficiencies is critical for successful radicchio cultivation. Integrated Pest Management (IPM) strategies, which combine biological, cultural, and chemical control measures, should be implemented to address pests.

To cultivate radicchio under the plant's natural growth cycles, it is essential to follow seasonal care guidelines. Proper seedbed preparation and transplanting are important in the early stages of the growing season, as is adequate irrigation during establishment to ensure robust root development. As the plants mature, adjusting irrigation frequency and monitoring nutrient levels become paramount. Radicchio should be protected during the colder seasons.

In conclusion, meticulous execution of crop maintenance and care practices, including pruning and thinning, weed control methods, vigilant plant health monitoring, and adherence to seasonal care guidelines, lays the foundation for a successful radicchio cultivation venture. Integrating these concepts with precision and adaptability allows for sustainable production, increasing profitability and contributing to the overall success of radicchio farming enterprises.

CHAPTER SEVEN
HARVESTING RADICCHIO FOR OPTIMAL QUALITY

Radicchio, a versatile and flavorful leafy vegetable, reaches its peak quality when harvested with precision and care. The process involves a delicate balance of timing, technique, and post-harvest handling. This section delves into the critical aspects of determining the right harvest time, the techniques used during harvesting, and the subsequent post-harvest handling and storage practices.

Determining The Right Harvest Time

The optimal harvest time for radicchio is a critical determinant of its quality and market value. Radicchio develops its distinctive bitter taste and vibrant colors during the cooler periods of the growing season. Typically, the best time to harvest is when the heads reach full maturity, which is characterized by firmness and well-defined coloration. Monitoring the size and tightness of the heads aids in determining the precise moment of maturity. However, climate

Harvesting Techniques

Harvesting radicchio should be done with care to avoid unnecessary bruising or tearing of the leaves, as these imperfections can reduce the overall quality of the radicchio. Using sharp, clean tools, such as pruning shears or knives, minimizes damage to the plant and ensures a clean cut. Additionally, harvesting radicchio early in the day, when the

Post-Harvest Handling And Storage

Radicchio's shelf life and marketability are significantly influenced by its post-harvest handling. After harvesting, radicchio should be promptly cooled to maintain its crispness and slow down the degradation process. Immediate removal of field heat is critical, and this can be achieved by placing the harvested heads in cool storage or refrigeration. Maintaining a temperature between 32°F to 40°F (0°C to 4.4°C) is optimal to inhibit physiological changes that lead to decay.

To prevent compression and bruising during transportation, it is critical to avoid overcrowding the packaging and instead use sturdy, breathable materials like perforated plastic or ventilated containers that allow air to circulate while also protecting the heads from physical damage.

Periodic inspections for moisture buildup, microbial growth, and changes in color or texture help maintain market standards and consumer satisfaction. Regular monitoring of stored radicchio is essential to identify any signs of deterioration promptly, and removing damaged or decaying heads prevents the spread of spoilage.

To summarize, successful radicchio cultivation extends beyond the field into the complexities of harvesting and post-harvest management.

A thorough understanding of the factors influencing harvest timing, the implementation of gentle and precise harvesting techniques, and meticulous post-harvest handling are essential elements in maximizing the quality and profitability of radicchio cultivation.

CHAPTER EIGHT
ADDING VALUE TO YOUR RADICCHIO

Radicchio cultivation not only provides an opportunity for agricultural profit but also offers avenues for adding value to the produce through various processing and packaging options. Utilizing advanced post-harvest technologies, such as cold storage and controlled atmosphere storage methods, can extend the shelf life of radicchio, ensuring a consistent and fresh supply throughout the year. Additionally, exploring vacuum packaging or modifications

Creating Unique Radicchio Products

Incorporating radicchio into innovative culinary products can be a game-changer for growers seeking profitability in the competitive agricultural market. Experimenting with various radicchio varieties, each with distinct flavor profiles, textures, and nutritional attributes, not only caters to varying consumer preferences but also allows for market differentiation.

Marketing Strategies For Value-Added Radicchio.

To successfully introduce value-added radicchio products to the market, effective marketing strategies are paramount. Understanding the target audience and their preferences is crucial. Conducting market research to identify consumer demographics, preferences, and trends can inform product development and marketing approaches. Leveraging digital platforms and social media can be instrumental in reaching a wider audience. Engaging in storytelling about the journey.

Sustainable Radicchio Farming Practices

Organic Radicchio Farming

Organic radicchio farming has gained significant traction in the era of increasing environmental consciousness.

Adopting organic practices not only aligns with consumer preferences but also contributes to the overall sustainability of agriculture. Using natural fertilizers, such as compost and manure, promotes soil health and reduces reliance on synthetic chemicals. Crop rotation techniques minimize soil degradation and pest infestations, enhancing the lo.

IPM (Integrated Pest Management) for Radicchio

Integrated Pest Management (IPM), which combines biological, cultural, and mechanical control methods to manage pests while minimizing the use of chemical pesticides, is essential for sustainable radicchio farming. Beneficial insects, such as ladybugs or predatory mites, can help control pest populations naturally.

Monitoring and early detection of pests allow for timely

Water Conservation In Radicchio Crops

With global concerns about water scarcity, adopting water conservation practices in radicchio cultivation is imperative. Drip irrigation systems, which deliver water directly to the root zone, are more efficient than traditional overhead irrigation methods, minimizing water wastage. Implementing soil moisture sensors can provide real-time data, enabling growers to optimize irrigation schedules based on actual plant needs. Mulching, by covering the soil with organic material

CHAPTER NINE
FINANCIAL MANAGEMENT AND RECORD-KEEPING

Radicchio cultivation involves a variety of expenses, including seeds, fertilizers, pesticides, labor, equipment, and overhead costs, all of which must be meticulously tracked and budgeted to ensure a profitable venture.

Expense And Budget Monitoring

To maximize the profitability of radicchio cultivation, it is imperative to maintain a detailed record of all expenses incurred throughout the production cycle. Variable costs, such as labor and inputs, fluctuate with production levels, whereas fixed costs, such as land rent and equipment depreciation, remain constant. Using advanced accounting software or dedicated agricultural management tools can facilitate acc.

To ensure financial stability throughout the radicchio cultivation process, it is critical to implement a well-structured budget, which outlines expected expenses and allocates resources accordingly. This proactive approach helps farmers avoid overspending and allows them to allocate resources wisely.

Revenue Recording

Accurate and timely recording of revenue generated from radicchio sales is fundamental to financial management. Revenue recording involves documenting the quantity of radicchio sold, the price received, and the total income generated.

A meticulous record-keeping system allows farmers to analyze sales patterns, identify profitable market segments, and make informed pricing and marketing decisions.

Integrating technology, such as point-of-sale systems or online sales platforms, can streamline revenue recording processes.

Automation not only reduces the likelihood of errors but also provides real-time insights into sales performance. Maintaining a customer database can aid in building long-term relationships, enabling targeted marketing efforts and repeat business.

Evaluating profitability:

To gain a comprehensive understanding of their financial health in radicchio cultivation, farmers should look into financial ratios and key performance indicators (KPIs), such as gross profit margin, net profit margin, and return on investment (ROI). These ratios provide insights into the efficiency and profitability of the radicchio enterprise.

To make informed decisions that lead to long-term success, farmers must consider both short-term and long-term perspectives when analyzing profitability.

While short-term gains are important, long-term profitability necessitates a strategic approach.

Growers can position themselves for success in the dynamic agricultural marketplace by constantly evaluating and adapting their financial strategies. They can also look into diversification strategies, such as value-added products or organic certification, to increase the overall profitability of their radicchio business.

In conclusion, meticulous financial management and record-keeping are indispensable components of a successful radicchio cultivation venture. From tracking expenses and monitoring budgets to recording revenue and evaluating profitability, each step contributes to the overall financial health of the enterprise. Farmers can navigate the complexities of the agricultural business landscape by using advanced technologies, strategic planning, and continuous analysis.

CHAPTER TEN
RECIPES AND CULINARY USES FOR RADICCHIO

Radicchio, a versatile and nutritious leafy vegetable, has gained popularity in culinary circles because of its unique bitter flavor and vibrant color.

Understanding the culinary trends associated with radicchio is crucial for farmers and entrepreneurs looking to profit from its cultivation.

Culinary trends frequently dictate the demand for specific ingredients, and radicchio has found its place in contemporary cuisine as chefs and home cooks alike experiment with diverse recipes.

Incorporating radicchio into various dishes requires a nuanced understanding of its flavor profile and texture. Its bitterness can be balanced with other ingredients, and its vibrant color adds aesthetic appeal to a variety of dishes.

Chefs and culinary enthusiasts appreciate its versatility, making it a sought-after ingredient in both traditional and innovative recipes.

Collaborating with chefs and restaurants is a strategic move for farmers looking to maximize profits from radicchio cultivation.

Chefs often appreciate fresh, locally sourced ingredients, and establishing partnerships can lead to consistent sales.

Farmers can work closely with chefs to understand their specific needs and preferences, ensuring a steady demand for radicchio in the restaurant industry.

Collaborating with restaurants also provides farmers with valuable

CONCLUSION

Growing, caring, managing, and using radicchio for profit requires a multifaceted approach that goes beyond traditional agricultural practices. Understanding and leveraging culinary trends, incorporating radicchio into diverse dishes, and collaborating with chefs and restaurants are essential strategies for maximizing profits.

By aligning cultivation practices with culinary preferences, maximizing